Gorillas

Victoria Blakemore

vblakemore.author@gmail.com

Copyright info/picture credits

Cover, andamanec/AdobeStock; Page 3, lElisal/Pixabay; Page 5, skeeze/Pixabay; Page 7, Alexas_Fotos/Pixabay; Page 9, 12019/Pixabay; Pages 10-11, emuturi/Pixabay; Page 13, Tony Northrup/AdobeStock; Page 15, Alexas_Fotos/Pixabay; Page 17, Alexas_Fotos/Pixabay; Page 19, jtplatt/AdobeStock; Page 21, mtanenbaum/Pixabay; Page 23; Erni/AdobeStock; Page 25, uzuri/AdobeStock; Page 27, Pexels/Pixabay; Page 29, Meldoraley46/Pixabay; Page 31, Williams_87/Pixabay; Page 33, andamanec/AdobeStock

Table of Contents

What Are Gorillas?

Gorillas are large mammals.

They are apes, not monkeys.

This means that they do not

have a tail.

There are four different kinds

of gorillas. They differ in their

color, size, and where they

live.

Male gorillas have a patch of

silver hair on their back. They are

called "silverbacks."

Size

Male gorillas can grow to be nearly six feet tall. They often weigh between three hundred and four hundred pounds.

Female gorillas are smaller. They grow to be about five feet tall. They usually weigh less than two hundred pounds.

The Eastern gorilla is the

largest kind of gorilla.

Physical Characteristics

Gorillas are black or brown in color. Their hair protects them from the cold and from insect bites.

Gorilla noses are all different. No two gorillas have the same nose. Researchers take pictures of gorilla noses to help identify them.

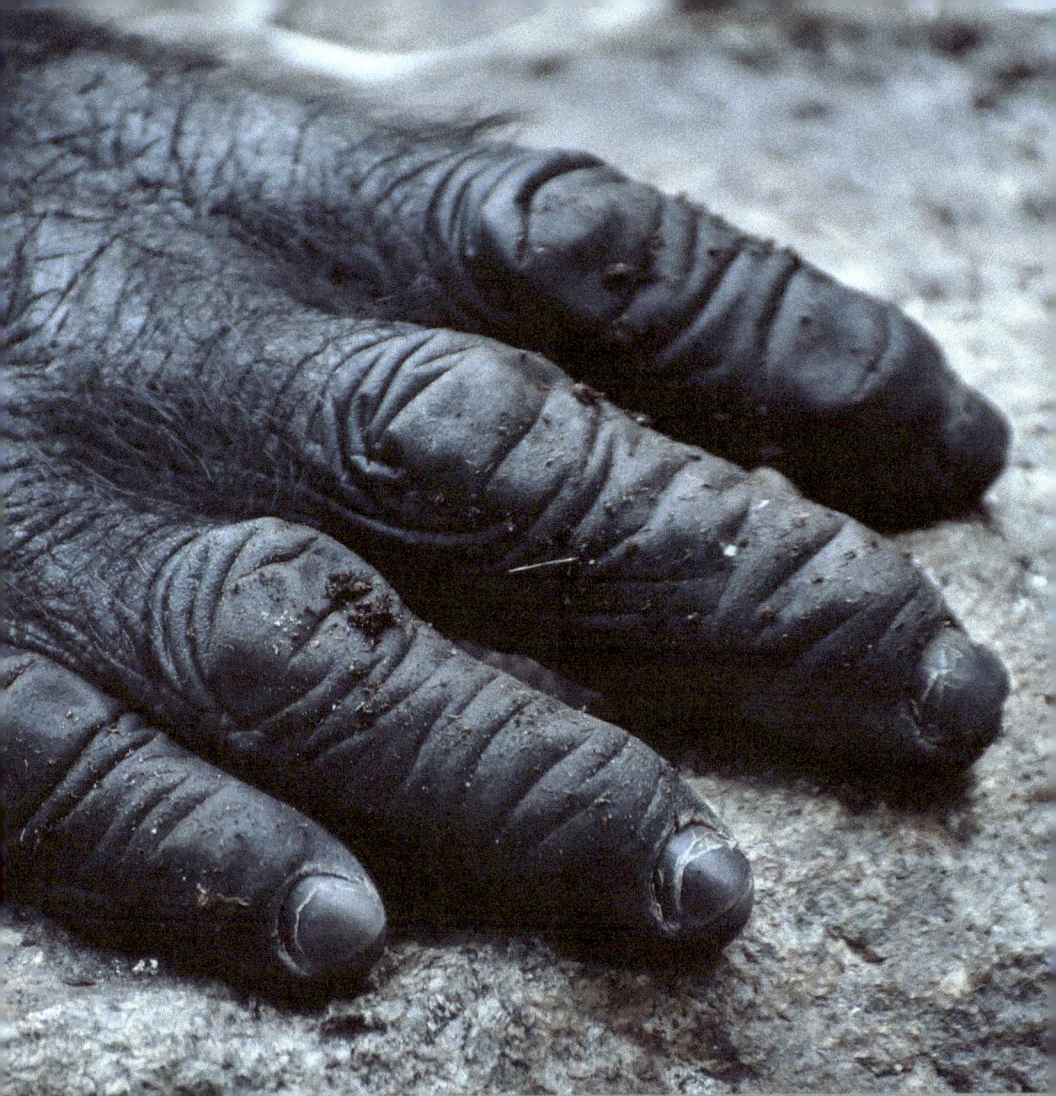

Gorilla hands are similar to human hands. They can use them to grip and climb. Their big toe is like a thumb. This also helps them to climb.

7

Habitat

Gorillas are found in the forests and mountains. Some may also be found in swamps. It can be very wet where gorillas live.

Gorillas need places with lots of plants. They need a wide variety of plants to eat every day.

Range

Gorillas are found in parts of central Africa.

They are often seen in countries

such as Cameroon and the

Democratic Republic of Congo.

Diet

Gorillas are **herbivores**, which means that they eat only plants.

Their diet is made up of leaves, shoots, vines, and fruits. They have also been known to eat the roots of some plants.

Adult gorillas can eat up to forty

pounds of food each day.

Gorillas are important to their ecosystem. Their **waste** works as a **fertilizer** for new plants. It can also spread seeds to different parts of the forest.

Gorillas have a very large stomach for an animal of their size. They need it to hold the large amounts of plants they eat each day.

Gorillas have strong jaws and
teeth that help them to eat
different kinds of plants.

Communication

Gorillas use mainly sound to communicate with each other. Sounds such as grunts, barks, whimpers are often used by gorillas.

Certain movements are also used to communicate. Male gorillas may beat their hands on their chest as a warning.

All gorillas use sound, but

silverbacks are known to be

very vocal.

Movement

Gorillas have longer arms than legs, which lets them walk on all fours. This is called a knuckle walk because they walk on their fist and knuckles.

Gorillas don't usually run, but when they do, they can reach speeds of up to twenty-five miles per hour.

They also have hands that are

similar to human hands, which

helps them to be great climbers.

Young Gorillas

Gorillas have one baby. Babies are able to crawl by the time they are two months old. They can walk by the age of nine months.

Baby gorillas ride on their mother's back as she moves through the forest. This helps to keep them safe.

Young gorillas often **imitate** other gorillas. This is one way they learn.

Troop Life

Gorillas live in groups of up to twelve gorillas. These groups are called troops. They are led by the oldest silverback of the group.

Young gorillas learn by watching the older gorillas in the troop. They also play-fight with each other.

Troops move to different places every day to find food. They sleep in nests they make out of leaves at night.

Intelligence

Gorillas are known to be very intelligent animals. Scientists have taught gorillas how to use sign language to communicate with humans.

One such gorilla is Koko, a lowland gorilla. She is known both for using sign language and having a kitten as a pet.

Gorillas can make and use tools.

In some places, they use sticks to

see how deep water is before

crossing.

Gorillas are **critically endangered**. There are not many left in the wild and they could become **extinct**.

There are thought to be fewer than 4,000 eastern gorillas left in the wild. There are fewer than 1,000 mountain gorillas left.

Gorillas can live up to thirty-five years in the wild. They may live as long as fifty years in **captivity**.

Gorillas in Danger

Gorillas in the wild face several threats. One of the main threats is that their habitats are being destroyed.

Young gorillas are sometimes caught and sold as pets. This is **illegal**. Other gorillas in their troop can be hurt or killed in the process.

Some people hunt gorillas for

their meat. Diseases like the flu or

the Ebola virus can also kill gorillas.

Helping Gorillas

There are many groups trying to help gorillas. Many groups focus on preventing habitat loss. Special **preserves** provide animals like gorillas with safe places to live.

In many places, there are laws that protect gorillas from being caught and hunted.

Conflict in countries where gorillas live has put gorillas in danger. Many people are trying to bring peace to these countries.

Other groups focus on research and education. They want to learn more about gorillas so they can continue to help them.

Glossary

Captivity: when an animal is kept by humans, not in the wild

Conflict: fight or strong disagreement

Critically Endangered: nearly extinct

Extinct: when there are no more of an animal left in the wild

Fertilizer: a substance added to soil to make it better for growing plants

Herbivore: an animal that eats only plants

Illegal: against the law

Imitate: to copy or mimic

Preserves: areas of land set up to protect plants and animals

Waste: material given off by the body after food is digested

About the Author

Victoria Blakemore is a first grade

teacher in Southwest Florida with a

passion for reading.

You can visit her at

www.elementaryexplorers.com

Also in This Series

Gray Wolves	Sloths	Flamingos	Camels	Koalas	Honey Bees	Pandas
Pangolins	White-Tailed Deer	Orcas	Giraffes	Corn	Meerkats	Echidnas
Walruses	Raccoons	Bald Eagles	Apples	Arctic Foxes	Red Pandas	Cassowaries
Tigers	Ladybugs	Moose	Beluga Whales	Leopards	Elephants	Jellyfish
Binturongs	Lions	Dolphins	Reindeer	Hammerhead Sharks	Hippos	Pumpkins
Peafowl	Chameleons	Florida Panthers	Aye-Ayes	Black Bears	Cheetahs	Manatees
Gingerbread	Polar Bears	Hot Chocolate	Orangutans	Coyotes	Marshmallows	Strawberries

Elementary Explorers

Victoria Blakemore

Also in This Series

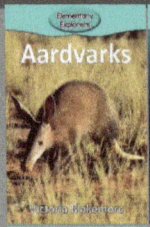

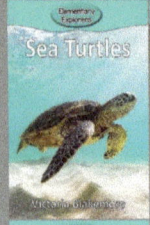

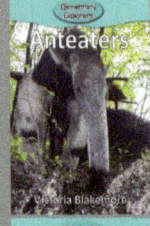

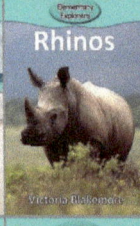

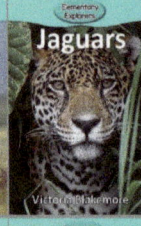

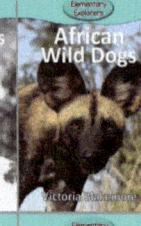

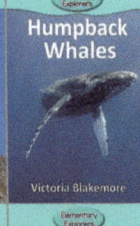

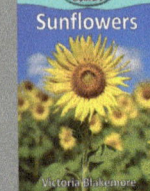

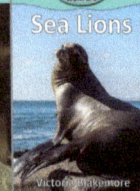

Aardvarks	Mako Sharks	Alligators	Frogs	Hedgehogs	Brown Bears	Bongos
Sea Turtles	Quokkas	Muskrats	Zebras	Red Foxes	Ring-Tailed Lemurs	Platypuses
Anteaters	Kangaroos	Rhinos	Jaguars	Wombats	Capybaras	Gorillas
Cats	Skunks	Butterflies	Dingoes	Snow Leopards	African Wild Dogs	Penguins
Whale Sharks	Wolverines	Warthogs	Caracals	Badgers	Seals	Hummingbirds
Pikas	Humpback Whales	Pumas	Lemonade	Llamas	Tulips	Ostriches
Sunflowers	Fennec Foxes	Sea Lions	Squirrels	Roses	Porcupines	Ice Cream

Victoria Blakemore

www.ingramcontent.com/pod-product-compliance
Lightning Source LLC
Chambersburg PA
CBHW051251020426
42333CB00025B/3163